Advance Praise:

Setting the Waves on Fire never ~~~ poetry. Arlice W. Davenport i~~~ writer, well-educated, well-read ~~~, a keen observer with an expansive heart and abiding passion for the English language. "In the sand, write with your finger a haiku," he says. "Make it jump like a frog into a pond of / lilies. Make it land on your heart." Davenport ranges the world from Cinque Terre to Lake Como to Chichen Itza to Cannon Beach. He brings each place to life, having become part of it: "A handful of soil would provide the perfect souvenir, *n'est-ce pas*? / sitting pretty on my mantle . . . like ashes spilled from a funerary urn, / the sacred remains of my travels."

Watch him pin today's headlines onto the fabric of history (from "Notre Dame Burns"): "Fire has done what revolution could not: / Our Lady has lost her head, flames so much / messier than the swoosh of the guillotine." In the poem "Shame" he takes on our shared burden, the accelerating retreat of the world's glaciers. "We swam against the tide / of *La Mer de Glace* . . . urging / the glacier not to turn back / from our carbon fin-print." His poetic influences and insights go back to Homer and Dante, forward through Rilke, Plath, Sexton, Harrison; from "Dream Song": ". . . John Berryman's wizened body shatters / on the frozen riverbed below Washington Avenue Bridge . . . Will this broken body be resurrected? . . . how terribly his faith has failed to trade // his daily delirium tremens for the *mysterium tremendum*."

This is poetry of intellectual breadth built on a foundation of honest emotional depth. I encourage you to take up this book and read, to follow Davenport's best advice: "Your heart is bruised, bleeding / drops of unrequited love. / The viscera of your body / tighten like a noose. You could slide // your head into it, if you choose, / . . . Love flees / like a deer bounding in a forest. / You are too broken to give chase . . . /. . . Let poems be your new heart. // It will not bleed."

— **Roy J. Beckemeyer,** Kansas Authors Club *Poet of the Year* and author of *Mouth Brimming Over,* his most recent book of poems.

In the second poem in his lyrical, luminous and sometimes terrifyingly beautiful first collection of poems, "*Setting the Waves on Fire*," Arlice W. Davenport has us "electrified by, / shivering with, transcendence." Van Gogh, Chagall, and Rilke are co-conspirators in this notion of the infinite that, as Edmund Burke put it, elicits delightful horror, while Rothko's ghost labors nearby, ironically stuck in Limbo because he did not believe in Limbo. In the final poem, we are left "still / seeking out transcendence, / still hungry for God."

Like Rilke, whose words open each section of this book of daily devotions, Davenport, too, is a seeker after awe and wonderment, something greater than oneself; realizing, like Burke, that the void, darkness, solitude and silence are necessary terrors along the road. In the end, after "waiting for Wordsworth's / daffodils to bloom," we are left contemplating that same poet's lament, "The world is too much with us."

Though he often sees "no way out," Davenport sings us through elegies on Basho's frog, D. H. Lawrence's tomb, a reverie for the author's father; lets us witness God guillotined at Cluny; Quasimodo "swinging on bells like a medieval orangutan" as "Notre Dame crumples in the wind, baptized / by the Holy Ghost and fire"; "The ghost of Victor Hugo" strolling "amid barricades of crime tape." Hope appears to have perished.

We stoop to pick a torn leaf from a mountain stream, Heraclitus' words echoing around us: "All things are in process." We pass "into light again," hear the "untranslated poetry" of the whale songs off the coast of Oregon, follow them south to Chichen Itza, where *El Castillo* stands, "perennially / built and rebuilt," where we stand, "alone upon the sacred causeway," and metamorphose "*to stone* – / the languid *chac mool*, / sated in sweet repose," until, at last, from "the porous depths," we hear "what it is to be called *human*." The ultimate transcendental epiphany.

This is a brilliant debut, fulfilling the promise of its title over and over. For the sake of your soul, do not miss this one.

— **Robert L. Dean, Jr.**, author of *The Aerialist Will Not Be Performing.*

Setting the Waves
ON FIRE

Setting the Waves
ON FIRE

POEMS
By Arlice W. Davenport

Meadowlark Press, LLC
Emporia, Kansas

Meadowlark Press, LLC
meadowlark-books.com
P.O. Box 333, Emporia, KS 66801

Cover Photo: Rob Greebon, www.imagesfromtexas.com
Riomaggiore, a major village in Cinque Terre, Italy.

Cover Design: Ron Muhlenbruch of Wichita.

ISBN: 978-1-7342477-7-0

Library of Congress Control Number: 2020942135

For Laura, as always

Table of Contents

waves: **SPIRIT**

waves: **WORLD**

waves: **POETRY**

waves: **BEING**

waves: **SPIRIT**

Let everything happen to you
Beauty and terror
Just keep going
No feeling is final
— **Rainer Maria Rilke**

Nearing the End

First, give all your money to the poor.
Then gather your other possessions
and burn them, breathing a prayer
of contentment as smoke spirals
to the heavens.

Write farewell notes to all your
dearest friends and nearest relatives.
Keep the notes clear and concise —
no euphemisms for death and dying.
No saccharine clinging to the world.

Find a reputable carpenter to build
a simple coffin — most likely
a plain pine box. Meditate on your coffin
for days, imagine yourself laid inside it
with no way out. It will be your temporary
home. Keep it sparse and Spartan.
Look beyond it to the void.

Ritually bathe your body — the last thing
you own — cleansing it of sin and regret.
Repent. Rejoice. Reunite with your Source.
Bask in the glow of requited love.

In the sand, write with your finger a haiku.
Make it jump like a frog into a pond of
lilies. Make it land on your heart
with ever the lightest touch.

Pray for grace to board your passage.
Only the living guess at its true nature,
unknowing on this side of the grave.
Read the *Phaedo* by Plato. There, Socrates says,

death is either a deep eternal sleep or
a reunion with other departed souls.
You do not have to choose. The reality
will come straight to you like a messenger
from afar. Be open to its meaning.

Finally, step into your coffin, fix the lid, and sleep.
When you wake, you will be on the other
side of dreams. Do not look back. You will
have entered the domain of the dead.
Make it your new abode. Clamber toward the light.

Angels

1.
The color fields shimmer
in yellows and blues.
Rothko's ghost lingers nearby,
wearing his snappy, green
editor's eye-shades,
studiously red-penciling
each word that a painting is not worth.
He labors in Limbo because
he took his own life,
even though he did not believe
in an afterlife, or in Limbo,
or in laboring endlessly
for redemption.

2.
The color fields waver
in primary hues.
You can see the suspended
movement in great
feathered rectangles, electrified by,
shivering with, transcendence.
Van Gogh believed in it.
So did Chagall: *Angels*,
on the order of Rilke's
terrifying beings from
a realm of suffering higher
than our own. They hear
our cries as a shimmering geometry
of color. Pick a hue, any hue.
Any hue will do.

Setting the Waves on Fire

The sea crashes hard into
the black boulders
of the harbor.
Fountains of spume dribble
landward into crevices.
Shrouded in gloom, I climb
slippery black stairs to spy
the spontaneous spectacle.

Rough sailing ahead.
Rough rains behind.

Cinque Terre craves attention.
Five Lands of building blocks
and pastel colors.
I stand on the slope
of indecision, stumbling
toward the rocky marketplace.

Can I buy peace there?
Can I set the waves on fire?

Riomaggiore anchors my fall
onto the watery stones,
black and blind.
Facedown,
I float the Five Beauties of spume.
It is safe among the crevices.

Wrestling the Flesh

1.
The flesh must be subdued,
for it cuckolds the mind
with its gargantuan girth.
To resist it we need clear reason,
not dark desire; myriad ideas,
not the anarchic imagination.

The weight of finitude
bears down upon us like
a vertical vise. We spread eagle,
arms outstretched, raised in
a straining V to stop
the mechanical pressure
from crushing us.

We will not die from this ploy.
But the weightless will no longer
fight back. The struggle, eternally
repeated, exhausts both flesh
and mind. Ideas still carry
the heft of conviction; yet
they barely move the needle
on the scale.

2.
Movement springs up like
a desert miracle.
Powerful leg muscles find

nowhere to turn but endless
rock and sand. The sky
offers no help: as empty as
the listless day. Clouds
pull apart like puffs of
moistened cotton;
they cannot mend the
empty self, for they themselves
need mending.
The flesh plays a shell game
with lust and love. Divine the
winner, then slap away any
sleight of hand that might
lead you astray.

3.
I wander the arid byways
of New Mexico; one road
leads straight to the tomb of
D. H. Lawrence. He took
more than his pound
of flesh; his blood
pumps an irrigating flow
into English literature. Flesh
turns to word in his mind.
And like a phoenix, it sprouts
wings and soars breathlessly
into the stratosphere,
far above the dusty canyons
and the dry arroyo of desire.

Shame

1.
We carry a river of ice within us.
Marred by dirty scuffed ripples,
like a starving child's ribs.
It ascends the mountain slope,
strewing in its wake a palette
of naked rocks and clear-cut tundra.
Orange-stained cairns point to our shame.

2.
Once you could see the glacier
behind the rough-hewn pulpit
of the tiny Anglican Church
on the South Island
of New Zealand.
Angelic white, full and overflowing,
the glacier swept into the front pew
like the descent of the Holy Ghost.
Now you glimpse only a dull tableau
behind the big picture window.
Aging panes of glass point to our shame.

3.
We swam against the tide
of *La Mer de Glace* near
Chamonix, France, urging
the glacier not to turn back
from our carbon fin-print,
urging the train we rode in on

to let us hike our way home.
All was silent except for
the constant drip, drip, drip
of *la Mer's* tears. We wept, too.
Centuries of history point to our shame.

The Living Self

1.
Memory blankets the past
in a neon green meadow
dappled with gray bits of matter.
They ooze and coalesce into a brain
brimming with unconscious narratives:
glottal globs clogging the gaps
of personal history. Tales of sound
and fury signifying nothing but the living self.

2.
The Transcendental Ego reigns over all,
smoothing the way for a unity of experience,
smoothing the way for a universe of sense.
I stroll alone through the empty patches
of meadow, waiting for Wordsworth's
daffodils to bloom. Waiting for poetry
to usurp the role of narrative, metaphor
crowned as the foundation of knowledge.

3.
The past besieges the present like Time's
Trojan Horse, teeming with shadows. At their edges,
light lines the darkness. To try to remember *now*,
the *tabula* is a noirish *rasa*, staring back
through dull, heavy-lidded eyes. *We see as we are seen.*
Memory dances before a mirror, a mirage so close
to our touch, yet so far out of reach. Starved for imagery,
we strain toward the black.

Stones

My father's legacy dies within me.
I carry his book of rules like a coffin with no lid.
A long, gray, wooden rectangle
full of admonition and praise,
phrases spilling out like stones
splashed with symbols and ciphers.

Stones stacked to heights below my grasp,
staging the play of ancient axioms:
Do, don't, resist.
Ahead, the future, rife with signs:
Go, stop, resist.
Resist the emptiness of death,
the ephemera of memory.

Carry stones like sins.
Pray for mercy, forgiveness.
Carry his legacy like iron
in the soul.

Weight of sorrow and disbelief.
Weight of anguish and grief.
Nothing good dies within me.

You Shall Live in Me

This constant vigil,
mercilessly endless,
is an act of love:
headlights blazing
through the broken dusk,
sickening heaps of flowers
crushed upon the seat.

Weighing down upon us
like handfuls of newly spaded earth,
begging to be tossed,
is the emptiness of endless tomorrows.

The smell of earth — warm and moist
and no one is there.

The mourners' tent is empty.
We have arrived too late.
Kneeling then, penitent, prayerful,
to touch the soil.

I trace my finger
over the epitaph engraved
on the hollow-white
headstone:

It is no longer I who live, but you shall live in me.

The limousine door
catches up the evening light.
Along the window's edge,
subtle hints of black and gray appear.

A long, soft cry
on the wind —
or is it the wind?

We answer back with our undying act of love:
You shall live in me.

No Other

(After Cavafy)

The sun flattens your vision
      to a wavering point.
            You search for a different sun.
                There is no other.

The wind stymies your breathing
      to an asthmatic wheeze.
            You search for a different wind.
                There is no other.

The sea shortens your journey
      to an anonymous port.
            You search for a different sea.
                There is no other.

The sky opens its vistas,
      vast, beyond your reach.
            You search for a different sky.
                There is no other.

The city blots your horizon
      with soot, smoke and ash.
            You search for a different city.
                There is no other.

The day dissolves in hours
    without number or name.
        You search for a different day.
        There is no other.

Beauty upholds its ideal
    like a statue without wings.
        You search for a different Beauty.
        There is no other.

The word pollinates the page
    with a frail, feeble sense.
        You search for a different word.
        There is no other.

The self mirrors the cosmos,
    a contracting black hole.
        You search for a different self.
        There is no other.

The poem laughs at your yearning
    for Art's Eternal Form.
        You search for a different poem.
        There is no other.

So you write the same poem
    from the same shrinking self,
        with the same weakling words,
            seeking the same ideal Beauty,

on the same day after day,
    in the same dirty city,
        under the same endless sky,
            beside the same aimless sea,

into the same stifling wind,
    blinded by the same soulless sun.
        And you call it a different life.
          But there is no other.

Losing Your Way

(After Cavafy)

Do not let your life get so far
ahead of you, busy and distracted,
that you meet it on the way back
a stranger, an alien.

Your years are long and vigorous.
They curl upon the sand
like S-shaped tidal waves, as the bay
seeps into the gray-green sea.

Tomorrow, if you meet yourself,
burdensome and strange,
you will have lost
your one chance for glory.

You will have lost
your way in a dark wood.
You will have lost
the mothering protection of the sea,

whose gentle tides are forever
taken away, never to return the same.

Tao

Ignore the Tao.
Mountains remain mountains.
Moon remains moon.
Infinity in a grain of sand,
raw silk, uncut wood.

Monk sweeps earthen floor,
mindfully makes jasmine tea.
Everything is as it always was.
All confusion shattered
in the clear light of being.

Ascension

1.
Angels with gossamer wings
flit heavenward
like bees nuzzling roses
for honeyed perfume.
I watch the angels flutter
higher and higher until
they grow smaller and smaller.
One of them looks back and says,
"You, too, will fly when the sinking
day darkens; when the moon
circles the Earth one last time."

2.
I think how I must free myself
from gravity, from finitude,
from time. The serious day
darkens. I watch it wriggle
into the sea, as infinite
as the sky, it seems, but a richer
shade of blue. The roses
eject the bees; their transparent
perfume wafts over me
from a mystical atomizer, particles
splaying my face, bathing my eyes.

3.
Beyond the sky, in ethereal Elysium,
the Immortals dwell. I gather my life

and cast it at their translucent feet.
They answer only in Greek riddles.
Oedipus wanders among them.
I am as blind as he, sinking into
a sea of shadows. Like a feathered
coral reef, wings waver over
the ocean floor. When the sated
day darkens, they will alight
on my back like petals on a rose.

Reading Li Po Aloft

Chinese master dreams
pink clouds trample bent grasses
ladders scale the sky

gray clouds tonsure peaks
glaciers flow in white rivers
nights drinking plum wine

clouds dream of Li Po
sky mountains spew fire and ice
tall trees touch the moon

waves: **WORLD**

I live my life in widening circles
that reach out across the world.
— Rainer Maria Rilke

Cluny

French revolutionaries guillotined God at Cluny,
but He exacted His tithe all the same:
one-tenth of their bad ideas tossed back at them.
The tyranny of terror, cheap dream of heaven, in ruins.

A vast emptiness swamps the nave;
stumps of pillars stained
black and gray and black again
by age and rain and blood.
Only one tower stands intact.
I scan the burnished hills behind it;
they do not look back.

"The birth throes of liberty," cries Thomas Jefferson.
"Rejoice!" Despots toppled; authority crippled
for a future that never comes.
Terror and waste, waste and terror.
The desolation of faith.

On the tiny town square, a bistro beams.
Syncopated lights surge behind the bar,
sending out distress signals of the mind:
the throb of synapses firing wildly in the wind.
Material infinity.

Old men saunter in to down a beer,
and harness their dogs under tables.
Parents and students sip pricey shots of espresso.
Emancipated energy.

Above the din, they cannot hear
the Earth's foundation crack.

Freedom leaves a sacred void in its wake,
watered by the blood of worldly martyrs.
On the menu: *égalité, fraternité,*
fissure and ruin.
Thunder in the hills.
Words crash around us like cannonballs.

Liberté lingers outside in the municipal lot.
A van propped up on wooden blocks for the night.
No hassles, man. *Free parking.*
Let's hoist another beer to Robespierre.
His dog strains at its leash.

Notre Dame Burns

Quasimodo frantically sounds the alarm,
swinging on bells like a medieval orangutan.
No sanctuary lingers in the smoldering nave.
Gargoyles roar like fire-breathing dragons,
then cower in corners, confused.

Notre Dame crumples in the wind, baptized
by the Holy Ghost and fire. Passion Week
transvalues every value: The great reversal comes.
Centuries of history agonize on the cross; dreams
of resurrection snag on collapsing rooftops.

Once, French pilgrims navigated by the spire.
Now it tumbles in flames, puncturing the pews
and all signs of hope. Prayers smother in the
    billowing smoke.
Non-believers gasp in hellish horror, while
the devil laughs, looting their scorched patrimony.

The ghost of Victor Hugo strolls amid barricades
    of crime tape.
Fire has done what the revolution could not:
Our Lady has lost her head, flames so much
messier that the swoosh of the guillotine,
strewing collateral damage in their wake.

The Outpatient Season

Warm and tender, the *sotto voce* passages
of *The Passion of Joan of Arc* soundtrack
waft softly through the room,
replenishing the pre-winter glow
of a perfect autumn afternoon.

Deep yellows, oranges and reds line
the cracking, gray sidewalk —
beacons of the inexorable killing to come
in this, the quiet dawn of the outpatient season.

I have survived many such seasons,
thinking only of what lies ahead,
willing myself blind to what has come before,
trying to grasp what is here, now,
dream upon dream upon dream.

I flee Time, the incorrigible executioner,
who leads each brilliantly colored leaf —
its medical gown gaping — to the lip
of the abyss, forcing it, with
an icy hypodermic shove, over the edge.

At the bottom lie piles upon piles of
fading badges of courage — oak, maple, elm;
crumpled prescriptions;
fraying prayer flags once flown to protest
Nature's annual euthanasia.

Now, in this outpatient moment, let us not forget
the sap of the trees slowly freezing,
let us not forget the mesmerizing harmonies
of angelic anthems urging us to turn away
from the illusory beauty accompanying death.

But let us hear the moans of Joan of Arc
as she is burned at the stake for heresy,
the flames leaping as high as her crudely
shorn head, singeing away her wispy eyebrows:
she, the chief victim of ecclesial euthanasia.

Yes, this is the outpatient season,
the season where autumn goes to die —
stripped, prepped and scrubbed —
and where we strive to survive,
in deep yellows, oranges and reds.

The Wine-Dark Hill

The vines have turned the color of the season —
as red as the wine their grapes will spill.
I peer back up the hillside into the circling sun,
an infinite swath of yellow. Below it surges
Homer's wine-dark sea, repeatedly, endlessly, effortlessly
spreading. Except the sea is never red in Greece or Italy,
or even in France, where I stand amid a sea of wine-red
     leaves,
in silence, under the sun, holding back the flood of
     invaders below.

From the crumbling wall of the vineyard,
I survey the village of Riquewihr in all its medieval
     splendor,
gorged with tourists like an unfortunate goose
gagging on grain forced down its gullet:
foie gras for the shopkeepers, who crowd the cobbled
     courtyard
in all its cacophony and chaos.
"Sample a macaroon for free under the ramparts."
"Buy a reproduction of a one-of-a-kind watercolor of the
     bell tower,
built in 1291. (Only 400 Euros for the original)," the artist
     says.
"Reserve it now for Christmas."

His stocking cap needs cleaning, I think.
I eye the village fountain, the half-timbered shops, the
     claustrophobic

stone houses, brightly painted, squeezed into walls like tiny
    fortresses.
The artist tells me how hard it is to make a living —
the global economy his impenetrable wall, which holds
    back a flood
of buyers from Germany, China, New York.

I decline his offer and climb the steep hill out of town,
the wine-dark hill of the vineyard.
This is what it means to inherit the world:
to stand apart, high, distant, above the sea
of other tourists, just like yourself, who yearn to stand
    apart,
just like yourself, laden with bulky guidebooks,
just like yourself, looking for the rarest souvenir, just like
    yourself,
the one that will sit elegantly on their mantle. Just like
    yourself,
they seek a memento that will remember for them —
    remember
all they could have had if only they had had the village
    to themselves.
If only you had had the village to yourself, to make it your
    own.

On this sunny afternoon, the village *is* my own — for a
    moment,
from a distance, awash in gray-blue shadow. Only the
    vineyard beams:
isolated, fecund, teeming with dreams; ever gaining on
    the harvest;

angling closer to the giant wine press that will spew
    the scarlet juice
at my feet, the earth turned the color of blood.
I resist the urge to pluck a baby cluster of grapes, nestled
    safely
beneath a leafy wave of this wine-dark sea, these purple
    berries
springing from the ground: so many earthy bubbles, born
    to burst.
Le terroir in French: The dirt makes all the difference.

A handful of soil would prove the perfect souvenir,
    n'est-ce pas?
sitting pretty on my mantle. The dust and debris would
    blow away
day by day, like ashes spilled from a funerary urn,
the sacred remains of my travels.

Let me be buried, then, in memory of the fertile furrows
    of Alsace.
Let me push up this hillside, along its ample paths
    of abundance,
its ripening rows of fruit, its wine-red passageways
    through leaves
and vines, steep and luminous, the sea of blood yet to be
    pressed
from the soon-to-be-crimson grapes.

"Does this vast vineyard hold any secret worth journeying
    halfway
around the world to find?" That is the question I scribble in
    the dirt.

"Does this village? Does this vision? Does this ancient,
   failing wall?"
Even if the answer is "No, no, no," I shall reply, "Yes, yes,
   yes."

Yes, let me be buried in Alsatian soil as a lasting souvenir.
Yes, let me lie here, as I stand: free and upright,
lighted by the autumn sun, unchanging, set apart
to revel in the marvel of red blood seeping into the soil.
Yes, let me make this stained patch of dirt my own.

The vines have turned the color of the season —
wine-red, wine-dark, blood-red.
And I have turned the color of the vines,
in silence, under the sun, holding back the flood.

All Things Are in Process

A single leaf,
nearly two-thirds torn,
floats idly down a mountain stream,
passing from light into darkness
into light again.

Refracted through the crystalline currents,
a bed of smooth, staid stones
cries, "Eternity! Everlasting!"
but the leaf drifts on.

And I, splashing my way upstream,
thinking myself the keeper
of this shadowed domain,
bend hurriedly
to pluck the leaf from my path.

Then, for just a moment, I hesitate,
to listen as the rivulets
lap against my legs,
longing to hear in them
Heraclitus' lonely, elegiac lament:

"All things are in process;
nothing stays still.
Upon those that step
into the same rivers
different and different waters flow."

But only the rocks sing on —
their same, unchanging song
of the stream's secret source.

And though I,
still deaf to their cry,
hear but the half-uttered echoes
of my fleeting thoughts,

I can see,
as the radiant flux of the night
again turns the leaf into light,
how at last we, too, shall step
into that same river twice.

At death —
when in the new-found *kenosis* of time,
all will be one.

(**Note:** "Kenosis" is a theological term that means self-emptying. It's usually applied to the incarnation of Christ. But I mean it in a more existential sense, of our — and time's — self-emptying at death.)

The Sea's Sacred Cleansing

heavy yellow-gray-lined waves
of fickle wrinkled tides
suck steadily at the runner's knees
foaming at the ankles
deep green and lathered
in the sweeping middle distance

he sweeps the rise of sand
and sedge with arms outstretched
eyes afloat
fingers ply flesh along his back
brush water from his legs
the sheeny stinging film of brine

the white beach runs a sweeping course
swirling with sand
drowsing in the drunken sun
he finds refuge this luminous blue
screeching of the soaring gulls
thunder of the surf

great black rocks divide the tide
rolling in fields of azure
limitless integral
he calls the sky
sweeping back
upon the distance
the endless sweeping middle distance

sunlight dazzles complexities of colors
ascetic flashings in richness of form
purity of beauty in fragrant elevation
the brine the sand

swept away running
for the purely accidental
the happiness success
of the accident of nature

movement in rhythm swift in apprehension
swiftly toward the integral combination
to combine the elements
fundamental the intensity
the brine the sand
the sea's sacred cleansing

Cannon Beach

I walk along Cannon Beach at low tide.
The sea lazily laps my legs.
The tawny sand is firmly packed, pockmarked
by seagull prints: birds on the hunt for food.
Tiny crabs scurry past. Orange-pink
starfish cling to black boulders,
plump, distorted sea creatures
inured to the tidal pull.
A lavender-red sky signals twilight.
I head toward Haystack,
natural icon of coal-black stone.
Ahead the path is strewn
with footprints.
I scan the horizon, alone.
Edified, I make
my way back home.

Whale Songs

Like Leviathan of old,
the rough, angry ocean
pummels the basalt shore
and coughs up its denizens
of the deep.

California Gray Whales
breach the surface of
the autumnal Oregon waters, slide
over the waves like seals
on the hunt,
their colors mingling perfectly
with the yellow-tinged whitecaps,
their bodies aimed perfectly
at migration south.

How innocent they sound
as their songs penetrate
the cacophony of the
crashing surf.

How magnificent they sound:
untranslated poetry, haunting
love lyrics, caressing
the beloved with a sonata
of sonar.

Like a child, they sing for joy,
and the sea turns a deaf ear.

But I hear them, and am transfixed
by their emotion and intelligence.
They sing to me, a mammalian
serenade at dusk.

I dare not sing back
for fear of failure. Of foolishness.

Yet I weep to hear them sing again,
once more before their majestic
passing to the milder seas of Mexico.

Chichen Itza

Like a stroke of genius,
of just plain blind luck
rising from the jungle floor,
the majestic rubble of the Maya calls,
at once the founder and judge of all Time.

First as the serpent whose plumes turn to wings,
then as the eagle boldly eyeing its prey,
and *en fin*! as the jaguar, sinewy and sleek,
El Castillo looms
against the hardened, sunbaked sky —
the shifting citadel of *Kukulcan,*
its shadow splayed across my days.

All of them numbered,
all of them too short,
all of them fading
in the cold, hard light of distant failure.

Perennially
built and rebuilt,
like the Church,
El Castillo stands
to meet the need of holy obligation,
to meet my need for initiation,
bounded only by the firmament and the underworld,
final triumph of the dead.

And so I will stand,
alone upon the sacred causeway —
enervated, unenlightened,
the bitter taste of dust in my mouth.

Until I, too, will be turned
to stone —
the languid *chac mool,*
sated in sweet repose.

I will drift toward the sunken *cenote,*
drink deeply from its oasis of evening cool,
where the memory of man and grain and god is sung:

an anthem of order, power and vision,
the great Mayan hymn of meaning.
I will hear, at last, from the porous depths of Yucatan,
what it is to be called *human.*

— *For Norman Carr*

The Ways of Barcelona

1.
Penitent pilgrims pack
the width of *Las Ramblas,*
marching headlong
down the pedestrian boulevard
toward the burgeoning square
of *Cataluyna,* scurrying
to find fountains and buses
to whisk them away
from themselves.
The burden of identity weighs
heavily in each backpack and bag.
I share their plight:
the onus of being.

2.
The sun brilliantly burnishes
the crowd, beaming with
a childlike hunger for toys.
Nothing changes
except the country
beneath their feet.
Tourism is purgatory
to the undirected.
No map, no plan, no
rescue from impulse.
Lacking travel's baptism
of fire and freedom,
they learn all roads

lead home
whence they came.

3.
Before the closed
doors of the cavernous cathedral,
Catalans circle, lift arms,
hop, twirl and dance.
Raised hands
signal unbrokenness.

Separation plays a different melody,
sends an inferno of deconstruction
spiraling downward, singeing factions
of language and race.
Yet a divided Spain paints
its face as united,
coyly cooing behind
a splayed, perfumed fan.

4.
I cool my heels at
the statue of Columbus,
anchored harbor-side;
the navigator
still ready to sail
under mistaken,
prevailing winds.
The crew
still ready to plant Spain's
contagion-carrying flag

in the shallows of faux India's
once purifying pool.

O America!
How far you have drifted
from these tapas bars
and tainted streets.
How far from the graffiti-
filled neighborhoods.
No space uncovered:
The gritty lust for color, figure
and form conquers all.

5.
All is exotic in
Mediterranean Barcelona:
the languid light,
the briny breeze, the sun
radiating like a silver
grapefruit in the azure sky,
the orange shards of tile
piecing together the face
of heaven.

Gaudi still erects his towers
in wavering waves of
nature and faith.
Inside *Basilica La Sagrada Familia,*
construction workers
hammer his corner
of paradise slowly into place.

Christ hangs naked
on the Cross.
A blue light filters
through *modernista* stained glass,
falls on the floor,
bathes my feet.

Piazza Navona

Bernini's sculptures float
over fountains like
a ship's mast set in stone,
straining to stray off-course.
I follow the muscular, hysterical
flow of the Four Rivers.
Lethe bubbles underground.
Step lightly.

Chubby-faced children spew
showers between their cheeks.
Nothing is quiet in Piazza Navona,
spreading to the seven hills
like a blanket of bedlam.
Heaving waves of tourists
speak to themselves in tongues.
Whose gift to Roma is this?
The Four Winds? The spigots spilling
holy water onto the hordes
of heedless souls?

Neptune stares down on
my dampened bald spot.
I will Photoshop it out
if he snaps my picture.
Or some petite, American tourist
will, craning her head
like a dolphin
flopping on Neptune's trident.

Navona is a nova of marble
and foam. Specters live here.
They shout here, they circle.
Bernini's spawn.

The Sea

(*After Elytis*)

1.
The sea lies leagues away.
I look leeward and see
no sandy beach, only this
sandy soil in which our plants
and flowers struggle to grow.
There is no sign of salty air,
or seagulls, or dolphins,
or seashells. No Neptune and
his entourage to capture
my weakening sight
with his flashing trident.

2.
How easy the Greeks had it:
the sea,
wine-dark, vast, the press
of tides calling the long
boats toward Troy.
Black mountains rise up
in a morning splayed with
iridescence.
Thunder and echo sound
in the warmth's embrace.
Glory gilds the waves.

3.

Today, the sea refracts
an aquamarine blue, lapping
against island shores,
which cradle the waves,
then thrust them back,
vivifying, in their
rhythms, the words of
infinity, singing
the endless song of the sun.
The spume
baptizes island souls
as the source of all life.
That is a lie, of course.
Or, shall we say, a myth.
Human life began on
the African savanna,
leagues away from the sea.

4.

Yet we need our myths
to fortify our dreams,
an irresistible radiance
clinging to the waves.
A heroic hymn
of exaltation. Bells
strike in the distance.
Yes, myths,
classical, traditional,
stretching toward the center
of things.

Crusading sails in
the current, carrying
our yearnings
for the eternal,
rosy-fingered dawn.

5.
Yes, we need the sea,
and its thrust-up cones
of stone on the horizon.
Freedom blows from all
directions, uncovering
great tales of destiny,
penitence, tragedy,
self-mastery, lament.
The sailor exults
in his salt-sprayed aims.
We need the sea,
wine-dark or blue, vast,
rough or tame.
Without it, civilization,
in all its majesty, infallibly
collapses.

6.
The sea lies leagues away.
I look leeward and see
only sandy soil.

Only Connect

The future swirls steadily
ahead, rocky, uncertain and dim.
Our choices are preordained
for freedom. We cannot
not choose. Creatures squirm
at the paradox. Black and white
no longer grace the color wheel.

Ragged caves beckon as shelter.
Birds take refuge in the tops
of empty trees. Exposed, they
chirp melodically at the moon.
There is no difference between
the road less traveled and its
counterpart. Mirror images,

they recede into the woods
at straitened perspectives.
I walk one alone, scanning
the sky for lasting signs
of the present. They are
blistered by sun spots.
The road veers inward.

Duration drags out time
to the breaking point.
What will be gestates
in what is. Seasons give
birth to a multicolored
brood. Sing them as a
cosmic anthem. *Only connect.*

Song of the Nightingale

The nightingale sings to itself.
Its melodious message flies
far from the bird's tiny tongue.
The song soars beyond her beak,
catches fire in another's nest.
Like listens to like; that is the mystic
chord of the rowans, in which singer
and listener unite, trading nuance
and beauty for nuance and beauty.
Only one self grasps this poetry:
the Oversoul of the seeping trees,
the hidden maestro of the music.

waves: **POETRY**

Find out the reason that commands you to write; see whether it has spread its roots into the very depth of your heart; confess to yourself you would have to die if you were forbidden to write.

— Rainer Maria Rilke

Dream Song

1.
Diaphanous dragons disgorge a deluge of diamonds
into the shadowed crevices of cumulus clouds.

Ruby-red sapphires overpopulate the glistening sky
like carbon-hardened locust: gorgeous messengers of
      the gods.

The Earth wears a crimson helmet, shielded from
the odious absence of ozone above the North and South
      poles.

Near Minneapolis, John Berryman's wizened body
      shatters
on the frozen riverbed below Washington Avenue Bridge.

Angels weep to see him jump, as he waves a vaudevillian
      goodbye.
The sapphires blanch, turn a violent violet. Black holes
      hover ahead.

2.
Shakespeare and Mr. Bones scat on mortality's skimpy
skeleton. Will this broken body be resurrected?

Does it deserve such distinction? Does its daring,
drunken destroyer? Four hundred *Dream Songs* sing yes.

Berryman toddles ticklishly toward the last traces
      of transcendence.

Love & Fame broadcasts how terribly his faith has failed
   to trade

his daily delirium tremens for the *mysterium tremendum.*
The God he prays to demands a syntax pure, plain
   and perfect.

With jolts of jest, He jimmies paradoxes into koans.
   Berryman
howls for a single diamond scratching the outline of his
   body on ice.

3.
He leaves a legacy larger than liquor, lechery and the
   love-struck ladies.
Lust seeds his fallow lacunae and lazily breaks his wife's
   heart.

Scholarship scoots him to the squeamish, secluded top
of his Shakespearean class: Signal student turns trusted
   teacher.

Poetry clones the Oklahoma clown in him. No successors,
no schools, no savvy peers, save Lowell, his fellow
   manic-depressive.

He dreams songs of hilarity, humility, history,
   dehumanization.
Poetry proves serious business until it learns to laugh
   at itself.

Sapphires crackle under the weight of the creaking
   sun.
They spin a kaleidoscopic rainbow of colors onto
   Berryman's obituary:

An irreplaceable jewel of the sky.

The Body of the Beloved

1.
Framed by a well-worn,
wooden windowsill,
we peer down on Purgatory
from our hotel perch
high above the restless shores
of Lake Como.

Behemoth slabs of marble
hang in limbo: rough-hewn
bodies awaiting their savior —
the divinely appointed sculptor
to chisel away the sins of their world.

Reflected in the window's wavy glass,
the ghost of Michelangelo
glides past — an aging slave to Beauty —
humming an Italian hymn to Venus
in syncopated rhythms.

He whispers that the stone
comes from Carrara,
carved out of ragged mountain sides,
carried down muddy, makeshift roads,
crated onto misshapen barges,
then barreled down the Arno River.

Last stop: Firenze.

2.
In his hands, marble beams
as the body of the beloved,
draped in splendor and light,
draped in radiant form — form
of the sculptor, not the sculpture,
of the Master, not the slave.

Beneath the rock-rough surface
of his métier, his soul
struggles to emerge from stone,
rising in rapture toward the Divine,
rising on wings of Beauty,
rising on wings of desire.

In his hands, marble melds into a mirror
of the making mind.
He levitates, an embodied Ideal,
rising higher, ever higher,
toward his immortal beloved —
yearning to be made real,
to be made flesh,
the "coarse and savage bark"
of the artist's first act.

3.
We come late to all
high lofty things,
he wrote.

And so we peer at the pit of Purgatory,
into its dissonant, disturbing discovery

that Art cannot save,
that Art cannot rightfully claim the artist's life,
that Art cannot breach the infinite reach
of Divine Love.

What happens is what is real;
but what is real is what we make happen.

The only choice, then: to go down, down, down into stone;
down into the blood-stained marble;
down into the rough-cut corners of regret.
Inconsolable, sculpture crumples into dust.

First, the patina falls away,
then appendages and organs —
everything but the sightless sea-surge
of skin, the seamless sanctuary
of pagan heroes and gods.

4.
The Ideal — immensity, enormity, infinity —
ignites in unrequited desire. The heart strains in vain
to bear the weight of stone.

In Purgatory's pit,
the Master stumbles:
Art cannot save him.
The body of his beloved crumbles.

Chiseled above his tomb:
Ripeness is all.

Poems

Your heart shatters
like a plate of china
smashed against
a grungy tile floor.

Pieces scatter like spiders,
impossible to retrieve,
impossible to rebuild,
impossible to contemplate.

Your heart is bruised, bleeding
drops of unrequited love.
The viscera of your body
tighten like a noose. You could slide

your head into it, if you choose,
but what would be the use? Love flees
like deer bounding in a forest.
You are too broken to give chase.

Yet the heart yearns
for completeness;
it is the foundation
of all desire.

Like a baby's cry
in the night, the heart wails,
begging to be heard. Echoes
permeate the dampened air.

You must breed
a new heart, with new desires,
tightening it together with
a titanium plate. This wound

will not be opened again,
though it aches and aches
in your jaded memory.
Let poems be your guide, their love

is eternal, they seek the ideal,
they comfort the sorrowful,
their lines inspire the helpless mind.
They raise you above the broken pieces

of existence. You have the choice:
Live or die, wallow in remorse,
or claw your way out of your battered shell.
You can decide today: Let poems become your new heart.

It will not bleed.

My Muse

If I ever write a poem again, I will forsake my Muse,
that fickle, toying sovereign of my imagination, too often
leaving me empty-handed in my hour of need.
Her well of words runs dry, sinking woefully below
the water table. She makes me drink sand and call
it champagne. I stagger past her in disbelief.

So I will let my senses suckle me, source of lasting
sustenance, my mind expanding in the grip
of clairvoyant sight. Look: Black lines on a bone-white
page stand out in low relief like monochromatic
hieroglyphs with an indecipherable story to tell.
But I seek poetry, not stories, and will discover only
dusty metaphors and sunbaked images beneath
the bone-dry surface of this forsaken temple.

If I ever write a poem again, I will write it backward,
dedicating the ending to my vacant Muse, who will read
the finale as a beginning, if she deigns to read at all.
Does art replenish the hollow heart until it bursts
from overflowing fecundity? Do poems patch
the torn muscle? She says yes, of course, like a two-penny
palm reader, rubbing out lines from my inky hand
that do not fit her preordained paradigm.

A Muse befits the myth-eating Greeks as a source
of soul-craft and finesse, attuned to Orpheus' lyre.
We have spewed out myth to make way for fact—solid
as stone, empty as an atom, shifting with the great

quantum winds. My Muse wanders aimlessly through
the desert, in search of words, of music, of nourishment
for the penniless poet in his epoch of need. *Need means
want means lack means void means loss means anything
but fact.* Let us seek succor in the seeds of the senses.
Let us cast the mutating Muse to the vortex of the winds.

The Way of the Poets

Beware the way your forebears came,
dragging goods and cattle, horses
and wagons, whimpering children,
not nearly enough food or water
to cross the unforgiving mountain passes.
Destination unknown.

They mistook the rugged, rocky, drought-
ridden road for the path to the promised land.
What they found instead was a land
full of promise, but beckoning only to the prominent
few, who could survive without loss of pride
or prowess or precious blood.

But that is not your way. You are destined
for much finer things, unseen, celestial
things that repair and reset your
spiritual compass, and unfurl the map
of successive crossroads you must face —
the terror of angels, the awe of the
miraculous, the angst of self-overcoming.

Your home is not of earth or water,
but of the sky, its heliocentric emptiness
broadcasts a better way to wander
through the inevitable suffering of
humankind. A delicate, mindful way.

No, your home is of the sky
and of its stars in all their ancient glory.
Together they project a haven of words
to protect you from the elements
and from ambush by the
rash mountain climbers before you.

Theirs is not your way, no.
Yours remains the way of Li Po,
the vulnerable, venerated way,
the way of the poets.

Keats' Yearning

John Keats touched the heavens with his odes.
"Nightingale" sings immortal.
His ravaged countenance foretold
a font of genius mournful.
Poems in beauty the perfect mode
to pass through time's strait portal.
Worn down by consumption's bleak goads,
inspiring souls still mortal
to bear bright Poesy's hard loads,
and fighting death to chortle,
and crack high *mysterium's* code:
All art turns stained and woeful.
Keats' yearning leads us up high roads
that strain for all things hopeful.

Alabaster

(For Mary Oliver)

In winter much of the living hibernates.
The dead seek out warmth.
Birds sing only in treetops, serenading
the world beyond. Let us soar to it
on the white wings of your poems.
You have said that one day we shall
live in the sky, but our consolation now
is the green earth, draped in snow.
Our footprints fade as soon as the sun burns
    down.
You left us in brightness. All your poems
embraced goodness, love and light.
A blanket of feathers covers your grave.
Beside them, a silver pen shines,
the instrument of grace. You wrote
more than we could absorb, more
than our mediocre minds could imagine.
You blessed us with the whiteness
of wisdom. We yearn to follow you
and the tree-top birds into the sky.
For now, we must feed on your alabaster
poetry, nature's hidden calligraphy,
spelling out our names.

E. E. Cummings Revisited

1.
Edward Estlin Cummings
rode Buffalo Bill's watersmooth-silver
stallion
into my high school English class in 1971
and broke onetwothreefourfive lightbulbsjustlikethat
over my head

he was a forceful man
and what i want to know is
how do you like your blueeyed boy
Mister Poet

2.
E. E. Cummings
whistled
the

goat-footed
balloonMan's   tune
far
and
wee
in Just-
spring
and
i heard
nothing but
the world as puddle-wonderful

3.
e. e. cummings cut the tops off
his capital letters and i

stayed a little
person

l(a

le
af
fa
ll

s)
one
l

y

i never signed
            my name
                    in uppercase
                                again

Homage to "Skunk Hour"

1.
Minds break apart at midnight,
piece together in dreamless sleep.

Robert Lowell poaches pen-and-ink
drawings for *Life Studies*.
Sylvia Plath dons Ariel's red dress,
but loses Ariadne's thread.

Lowell raises *For the Union Dead*,
mythic monument to his family's best.
Pigeons decorate it with their fecal mess.
Plath pins a swastika to her chest —
shockingly pink —
and stands beside the kitchen sink,

stirring a pot of poet's gruel.
Madness and death the golden rule
no artistry can break. Not even the careless
reader can take leave of these senses

once they're rendered on the page.
Confessions don't age well,
as Lowell knows oh so well,

unless they suggest more substantial fare,
say, a flannel bathrobe for him to wear
in a Boston psychiatric ward — if he dares.

There's something wrong with his head.
Crown him Caligula; his lineage has fled.

"What does that have to do with me, Daddy?" Plath artfully
    whines.
"Fill the tulip jars with red water, not wine," he replies.
"The bridegroom cometh. Turn off the oven."
But it is too late. She has met her fate before it predeceases
    her.

Like a teacher's pet, she bets her life on a recitation
of *Daddy*, a term of endearment,
a term of interment in a stark, loveless miscarriage,
a dark, masculine disparagement of her freedom. *O Daddy
    dearest.*

Lowell shoots up to salute the younger poet, guessing
she has given the year's best reading by a girl in red
    dresses.

At this stage, what does it matter that his "mind's not
    right"?
What can he do but give up his right to pray, as every
    insight
slips away?

But no Our Father for Plath. For her, the Kingdom comes
    too late.
Colossal poetry cannot save; the poet raves and raves and
    raves
into that dark night.

Turn off the oven, turn out the lights. Daddy, too, is
    not right.

2.
Blake fired his Proverbs of Hell
in the dull, damning kilns
of England's Industrial Age.

A poet's no sage, but Lowell earned
his wings when he doctored Blake's phrase:
"I myself am hell."

A stone angel directs his descent:

Fortune favors the bold.

Never discount the power of chance.

Affliction of the senses is a gift.

Invisible seeks invisible.

Darkness obscures our limits.

We carry darkness within us.

Anarchy breeds spirit.

Artistry breeds no merit.

Appropriate beauty, at all costs,

whether, man, beast or angel.

3.
Poetry births an artifact of words; we unearth them, and
    they adhere.
We bury them, and they fall flat — hollow sounds, futile
    splats,
prehistoric grunts ground into the ground.

Bathed in lithium and alcohol, here bobs your calling,
    Robert:
Everything matters; nothing coheres.
Build a shell of a soul on this maxim, a notebook of
    negation.
Grind your axes.

Sanctuaries may crumble, gates may close. Press on.
    Press on.
Corkscrew your identity into the iambic line; rouse the
    reader to find
the misleading promise of Eternity in the sonnet,
    the sonnet,
the endless sonnet.

For minds lost in madness, tree limbs dangle like kite tails
    in the wind.
No one flies here anymore. Gather reddened kindling while
    ye may.

What exiles you from the ancients — Homer, Virgil and
    Horace —
springs from vision, not technique: You lack the requisite
    blindness.

Absence absents the soul. Here, now, forever, shimmers
    only presence,
only the present, only Presence: divine, human, animal,
    marmoreal.
Skunks, sails, cars and pails. Sing on, O son of New
    England!

Day by day, failing all, fill your void with fiery
hieroglyphs of verse. Then call your duty done.

4.
Behold: You are not the favorite, after all, but Camus'
    stranger,
trapped in the blinding sun, stumbling on the burning
    sand.

Only what dies in you endures.

"Is getting well ever an art,
or art a way to get well?"

The skunks scurry, scavenge and survive far too long
    for you to answer.

You lie down beside orange fishnets, facing the shore.
At midnight, you will dream of dreamless sleep.

Along the Forest Path

1.
You speak the word
that will hold back
death, muffled along
the forest path.
I seek a clearing
to hear keenly
what was said.
I seek an opening
to liberate all
meaning. Nothing
shows itself, save
the flittering of birds.

2.
The poem is not yours to keep,
nor the others, who so eagerly read.

It belongs to the earth,
fated for the forest floor,

sifted through mounds
of leaves, yellow and brown,

buried by a hiker's boot,
unwilling to be found.

3.
Poetry fortifies the bond
between spirit and breath.
Each verse an exhale.

Poems dwell in the forest,
thick, silent and dark.
Our hut hovers high in the sky.

There, exhales dissipate.
The word thins, death thrives.
And poetry mourns the final whimper.

Laurels

We die of ennui and enervation,
blind to the cosmos' resonating
with a revelatory repertoire
of marvels and wonders.

Our heart intermingles
with The Heart, history's unseen
force, pushing the dialectic
forward to its inevitable conclusion.

Art is no easy accomplishment.
The Muse descends in silence.
We listen for her secret command,
shaping words into the integrity
of the poem. The Heart imprints
our heart on the open page.

The Heart rises with our heart
to the realm of the Titans, muscular poets
crowned in laurels and draped in multicolored
sashes. They have shown how
willpower can decode the Muse's
cryptic command, how poetry
rises, eternally reborn.

We die of ennui and disappointment.
The cosmos enriches itself without us,
counting billions of stars, not hundreds

of poems. Consider the Muse as
the Delphic Oracle: *Ignore her at your
peril.* Follow her heart to the end.

She knows that glory awaits
the courageous heart of the poet.
She knows that there are
laurels enough for everyone.

This Is How the World Ends

(After Anne Sexton's "The Starry Night")

Van Gogh's "Starry Night"
illumines a damaged heart.
Poetry remains therapy
until the patient is cured.

Pulitzer Prize, parties, men
and accolades galore.
Anne Sexton, the poets' darling,
dances to the darkening sky.
This is how you want to die.

This is how the world ends:
without swirling stars,
without a crescent moon,
stuck alone inside your garage,
door closed, car running.
Inhale the aroma of the blackened night.

Palms

As I lie dying, I will write poems
on my palm, using a calligrapher's brush.
The ink will dry overnight.
In the morning I shall start again.

Li Po will sit beside me, reciting
poems about the moon and clasping his palms.
When I am gone, he will burn the ink and brush
and streak his palms in rich charcoal.

Finale

(For Jim Harrison)

poetry is no great solace
alone in my Montana cabin
with my faithful hunting dogs
who still don't know me by name
a bottle of 1976 Chateau Mouton Bordeaux
at my left elbow
a meal fit for a gourmand prince set before me
my back blisters in mutant patterns
of unease
there is no sun to burn them away
outside a three-day blow rattles
the hinges
a razor-sharp mountain trembles
the wind yearns for my undoing
i have unraveled my medicine bag
beads of healing scatter across the floor
one more manuscript blossoms
in the desiccated orchard
my heart gives way
slumped over my ancient typewriter
i fail to complete the final phrase

waves: **BEING**

Make your ego porous. Will is of little importance, complaining is nothing, fame is nothing. Openness, patience, receptivity, solitude is everything.

— Rainer Maria Rilke

San Pietro

Michelangelo's *Pietà* shrinks
behind glass.
Bernini's canopy shimmers
in wavy brown.

The sculptors face off
like boxers in a ring.
Each punch plants
a terrible dent in
white marble.
A squeeze of a hip here.
A dip of a head there.

Stone can wrinkle
like time. Light
can emanate from
wood, gilded
in geometric forms.

Death laps across
a mother's lap.
The divine turns human
in a litany of flesh.

Formless blocks of stone
ascend to the dome,
met by a descending dove.

Perfection in art.
Love bounded by love.

Beatitude

1.
William Blake's Ancient of Days
casts down atomic-yellow rays
of ever-shimmering light.

Coal-scuttled clouds vie
for dominion in the dusky sky,
winnowing to purple, to pink.

On the desert floor,
barren and warm,
recumbent dunes lie like sleeping women,
restless, shifting, breeding new form.

Images whirl in the whiplash wind.
Cacti stand sentinel over unspoken needs.

2.
All this passes for dream in my world,
a cosmic concatenation of identity,
a blueprint, a revelation, a tender embrace.

Secret impulses carry the dream
down the royal road of the soul,
which quivers in the dark, seeking succor.

Suddenly laid open, it lets energy pour in:
sacred, incumbent, a beacon of beatitude.

Eternity

The lighthouse looms
far off-shore.
Its blinding Cyclops eye
circles like a hawk
closing in on weary prey.

The beam blips to
eternity, signaling
wayward ships to slow
their progress through
choppy seas.

We have no paradise here, save
the spectacular Oregon coast
after sunset, when flat sand lights
up like a neon walkway and
purple streaks paint the sky.

Star fish, in puerile pink, cling
to black boulders. Waves
dive deep. The lighthouse
keeps signaling to no one.
No dust of eternity to be found.

Amor Fati

all is silence

jagged shards of light
fixed in endless desolation
strike sharply
against the sides
of motionless summits

the bruised, burned-over earth
catches up the windless morning
in a moment
red, translucent tides of blood
surge across the surface
retreating in salted wavelets

black fissures of stone
revile the thick, blind flood,
fall silent — abandoned —
in the pitiless, rhythmic
surging of the broken sky

you have entered the domain
of the responsible ones

out of the boundless, merciful darkness
of the yawning void comes
the howling wind of solitude
gliding on thin, clear wings
its precious appeal from space descending

upon the empty, ashen valleys
dark, secret murmurings left clinging
to your desiccated land

no singularly powerful bracing root
no spot of earth that is fruitful
the pale pink/azure sky
stands immeasurably high above
the burning plains
and everywhere you look:
dust and sand, dullness, languor and guilt

titanic violator
born out of time in chaos
your final strategy
must be changed

what have you inherited
but the superfluity of truth
the discord between
mystery and meaning
the black wisdom of the cosmos

in the distance
above the untouched landscape of loneliness
bright flames are quenched
in the boundless oblivion of heaven
it is not your own

even the silver shining vision
of the daybreak sky
has been stolen by you

the movement of history says
you are the guilty one

you have entered the domain
of the responsible ones
you will not be remembered

Apple Tree

We trundle down the wooden steps
behind the weathered farmhouse,
headed toward the orchard
planted in yellow grass.

Only one tree still bears fruit,
the others dried up from unwilling
neglect, the inheritance of old age,
the dark turning of nature's cycle.

Looking back at the westward window,
I see nothing but its vacant stare,
seeking the setting sun to reflect
its waning light.

You stumble past the lonely apple
hanging precariously above the ground.
When it falls, your legacy of husbandry
will be complete.

I glance into the dull glaze of your
ancient eyes, seeking a light to reflect
my image, hidden neatly in
the folds of your wrinkled face.

I am the only fruit left hanging
from your long, English lineage.
I snatch the wizened apple
and lay it lovingly in the grass.

It will wither with the winter winds.
Next to the sun's slanting beam,
I feel the frisson of autumn's chill.

Dusk settles on the fields.
I stare at your stooping frame,
my arm hooked precariously
through the tree's crooked branch.

— *For my father, 1922-2014*

The Dead

1.
The dead hover over their graves,
an unsteady flame flickering
wildly like an inferno.

We cannot snuff it out.
Kaleidoscopic shadows splay across the earth:
brilliant oranges, yellows, reds, and a fatal greenish-gray.

The colors inexorably build to a crescendo.
At midnight, a moldering movement begins:
the dance of resuscitation, brittle and dry.

I cannot dance, a lesson lost to the absurdities of youth.
Levity does not lead to levitation, anyway.
My feet are stubbornly stuck to the ground.

The dead despise the living, they say,
always chirping and harping on the day's
annoyances, dullness and anguish.

How soon the deceased forget their own past.
How desperate we are not to lose ours.
How uncanny when we meet, cheek to cheek.

The dead blame us for their failings and unrequited
desires. They reignite their flimsy flames,
mumbling, "Absolution." We mumble back, "All must pass."

2.
I flounder through Flanders Fields,
mourning the great fallen poets of The Great War.

So many sensitive yearnings skewered at the end
    of a bayonet.
So many bright, vibrant promises shredded by shrapnel.

Machine guns mowing down row upon row of militarily
    naïve
Englishmen. Red-hot bullets rain about their heads,

lodge in their eyes. All for God and country. The soldiers
    shed
their own colors: brownish-gray for the muck, dirty khaki
    for the clay,

trench green for the woolen uniforms, alabaster white
for the shocked, dying faces. Our mantra: "This, too,
    must pass."

But it doesn't. Generations of the living warm to
    the graveside
infernos, mumbling, "Absolution for all." The dead answer
    back: "Patience."

The Great Migration

Before the monsoon descends in feverish
torrents, and The Great Migration begins,
the earth crumbles, crackles and slides
into tawny showers of sand and stone.

Parched prey pray to elude their nemeses,
who scour patches of brown grass,
their noses low and quivering, sniffing
the dust for the faintest fragrance of food.

Baboons heckle crocodiles, whose eggs they've stolen;
female lions pounce on defenseless gazelles. Necks snap.
Life looms for all in the gathering rain clouds.
Yet death will follow, stealthy as a leopard in tall grass.

We tramp the globe like a shaky-legged newborn
giraffe, awkward and vulnerable, dewy-eyed and gulping
the heavy particles of air for the sure scent of sustenance.
Our prey carries no smell, no taste, no movements.

It is sheer spirit shaped from the eternal whirlwinds
of dust that dance around our path. How else shall
we advance? Rain, when it comes, only splatters
in our eyes. We await The Great Migration of Souls.

Mountain

Do not succumb to restlessness.
Another journey will not drain the ocean
or clean the sky.
Another mountain will not reveal
the rooftop of the world.

You have your own mountain within.
It pierces the sky, buoys on the sea.
Climb it in solitude, in inwardness.
Rest in exertion.

You will find adventure, joy —
a pilgrimage to heaven's gates.

Climb, climb, and you will find
the face of God.

Pyrénées

I had forgotten the way to the hut that I had traveled to so
    many times,
so many days. *So many moons,* I would say. But no one marks
    moons anymore,
except hunters. And I am not one of them. Nor a gatherer.
I listen to old men tell how they felled the stags. I do not
    believe them.

I am a wayfarer, to use the archaic words I used to love,
    the words
I had forgotten, the words of time in eternity, the words
    of orange leaves
on towering pin oaks, the words of circles of shadows
    settling on Gavarnie,
of snowfall in the Pyrénées. *Sever Spain from the Continent.*

I had lost the language of the dirty, spray-painted sheep
    scampering
over gray-bouldered cirques on mountaintops, boulders
    turning into
mountains in the shadows, in the fog, in drifts of snow.
    There are
no words for this now. Bleating sheep drown them out,
    and yapping dogs.

There are no words for the radiance of transcendence.
    "Climb higher,"
I hear them say. Higher into the haze of clouds. *Cirque: circle,*
    circus.

Acrobatics on hillsides, balancing acts on rockslides,
    skimming streams
in hard-toed boots. I had forgotten the way to the words,
    far behind me.

I have come to a gate, a steep stile in shadow. No sheep
    can pass.
Nothing looks familiar; nothing looks strange. I saunter in
    a cloud
of unknowing. I had known the words: worn, smooth
    as stone unmarred
by hard-toed boots, slick as snowmelt. *Slide from France
    into Spain.*

This is the path of Santiago de Compostela, the route of
    St. James, who said,
"Do not be double-minded, brethren." I cannot remember
    if I have been
double-minded in my travels. I had forgotten the way. If
    the words
do not come, which mind sees the threshold, which mind
    circles the fog?

What passes, what begins in wanderlust? I do not look
    backward.
The way lies ahead, waiting, winding away from
    the words. Splotches
of lichen sprout orange and green. "Go no higher for
    safety." *No higher.*
They do not mention exile or ecstasy or the straight path
    of radiance.

The cirque circles my words in mountain shadows. I must
  unlearn
my wanderlust, adrift in broken fields of stone. I had
  forgotten the way
to the hut. Rocks obscure the path. Light ensures the path
  leads upward.
Nothing is lost. Words hold their weight. Stags dance above
  me in fog.

Dasein

One hand in a field of diamonds,
the other slopping pigs.
You are neither star nor earth,
as Rilke would have it.

You are always *in medias res,* always
on the way, thrown into the world
toward some dark horizon.
Never settled, never open.

Never easy, never found.
Truth eludes you like a fugitive.
Your will evades everything
but pride. You run toward sunrise,

a being-unto-death. Now hisses
in a still small voice: *then.*
Here means elsewhere, there
means nowhere.

Turn back into the void. It taunts
you, tightens its grip on your gut,
spews smoke in your face.
You eat despair, regurgitate fear.

Where Titans swagger, you scurry
toward safety. You keep searching,
one hand in a field of sapphires,
the other trailing God.

(**Note:** "Dasein" is the German word for "being-there." The
philosopher Heidegger uses it to describe human existence.)

Horizon

On the flat edge of the horizon
a purple-pink glow beckons me on,
across empty fields dusted with snow.
Trees raise their hands in praise
for the end of this day, plump with possibilities.

I have accomplished nothing.
Yet I turn the lathe one last time,
cutting metal, cutting bone,
with a wound too deep to plumb,
too dark to lighten, transfused
with blood that stains the sun.

Sorrow trails me like a bird dog
sniffing out her prey, startling
quail to take flight. I watch them
pass overhead. I am not a hunter.
They are safe to flee, coveys of comfort.

"The world is too much with us,"
Wordsworth proclaimed. I contemplate
his lament, but see no way out.
Ancient faces watch my route —
I am aimless, famished, still
seeking out transcendence,
still hungry for God.

About the Author

Arlice W. Davenport was 17 in a high school English class when he read "In Just-" by E. E. Cummings. He was amazed at how words could bounce, skip and zing across the page; how the poet could twist and turn spacing, punctuation and syntax to create an innovative meaning that was intentional, straight from the heart.

He knew that this, too, was what he wanted to do with language. And he has been writing poetry ever since — although his poetic forms and sensibilities have matured beyond a 17-year-old's awe. Still, that awe sticks with him. And he has never signed his name in upper-case.

Davenport, a lifelong Wichitan, is the retired Travel editor and Books Page editor for *The Wichita Eagle*. With his wife, Laura, he has explored Europe more than 30 times. He has had poems published in the (erstwhile) *Osage Review, River City Poetry,* and on AllPoetry, the world's largest poetry website. This is his first book of poems.

Acknowledgments

I owe deep thanks to the following people:

Bob Dean, an extremely gifted poet, for his initiative and encouragement in editing my poems and in getting this project rolling. There would have been no book without his vigilance and belief in me.

Roy Beckemeyer has been my inspiration from the time I joined Kansas Authors Club. His legacy of being KAC's *Poet of the Year*, and his tireless creation of new, innovative poems sets the highest standard for any Kansas poet. Perhaps someday, I might creep closer toward it.

Tracy Million Simmons has proven to be the most gracious and knowledgeable publisher *par excellence*. Her immaculate work ethic and drive for publishing excellence has made it an honor to collaborate with her on my debut book of poems. I can think of no one else who could have produced such a lovely book. I am proud to be an author for Meadowlark Press.

Finally, my wonderful wife, **Laura**, has remained steadfast and patient, understanding my obsession with (near) perfection in words and design. She has indulged my long nights of writing and being anchored to my laptop. I send her all my love. She more than deserves it.

Publisher of Fiction, Memoir, and Poetry Since 2014

Home of The Birdy Poetry Prize

meadowlark-books.com

Made in the USA
Columbia, SC
24 October 2020